PROFESSIONAL DEVELOPMENT

Unleash Your Potential in the Modern Workplace

Ray Goodwin

ISBN-13: 9798852987716

Cover design & images by: Ray Goodwin

CONTENTS

LIABILITY DISCLAIMER

The information contained within this book is intended for informational purposes only and should not be construed as legal or professional advice. The authors and publishers of this book are not responsible for any losses or damages that may arise from the use of the information contained within.

The reader assumes full responsibility for any decisions made based on the information in this book. The authors and publishers do not endorse any particular method, service or product mentioned in this book and are not responsible for any consequences resulting from their use.

The reader should exercise caution and discretion when making life changing decisions, and should be aware of the risks and potential consequences of their actions. This book is not a substitute for professional or legal advice and should not be relied upon as such.

By reading and using the information in this book, the reader acknowledges and agrees to hold harmless the authors, publishers, and any other parties involved in the creation or distribution of this book from any and all liability, claims, damages, or losses that may arise from their use of the information contained herein.

CHAPTER 1: INTRODUCTION

Welcome to Professional Development, a comprehensive guide to help you build the skills and knowledge necessary to succeed in your career. Whether you are just starting out or looking to take your current position to the next level, this book will show you how to develop a plan for professional growth that fits your unique needs and goals.

As someone who has been working in various industries for almost 30 years, I have seen firsthand the importance of ongoing learning and development. The world is constantly changing and evolving, and those who stay stagnant quickly fall behind. This book is designed to help you keep up with the pace of change and rise above your competitors by continuously improving your skills.

In these pages, you'll find practical advice on everything from setting career goals and identifying gaps in your knowledge, to networking effectively and finding mentors who can guide you along the way. You'll learn how to communicate with colleagues more clearly, manage conflict more effectively, and develop leadership qualities that inspire others.

Let's Begin

As we navigate through our careers, we often find ourselves seeking ways to progress to the next level. Whether we want to advance in our current positions, change careers, or start our own businesses, one thing remains constant - the need for professional development.

Professional development is an ongoing process of learning, growing, and expanding our skills and knowledge of our chosen profession. The benefits of professional development are numerous and range from personal growth and satisfaction to increased job opportunities and earning potential.

In this guide, we will explore the different forms of professional development, why it's important, and how you can create a plan to improve your skills and advance your career. From assessing your needs and setting goals to networking and developing leadership skills, this guide will offer practical advice on how to enhance your career prospects.

The Different Forms of Professional Development

Professional development comes in many different forms, from formal education programs to self-directed learning. Some of the most common forms of professional development include:

❖ Formal education: This can include degree programs, certification programs, and continuing education courses.

❖ Conferences and seminars: Attending industry-specific conferences and seminars can help you keep up with the latest trends and technologies in your field.

❖ Webinars and online courses: These can be a convenient and cost-effective way to learn new skills and stay up-to-date without leaving your desk.

❖ Mentoring and coaching: Working with a mentor or coach can help you gain perspective on your career goals, identify your strengths and weaknesses, and receive guidance on how to move forward.

❖   On-the-job learning: This can include shadowing colleagues, taking on new projects, and learning from experience.

❖   Networking: Developing relationships with colleagues and industry leaders can offer valuable insight and job opportunities.

❖   Reading and research: Staying up-to-date on industry publications and research can help you identify new trends and techniques and stay ahead of the curve.

The Importance of Continual Learning

Professional development isn't a one-time event. It requires commitment to continuing growth and learning throughout your career. In today's fast-paced and constantly-evolving business landscape, it's crucial to stay up-to-date with industry changes, new technologies, and emerging trends.

Continual learning not only helps you stay relevant and competitive, but it also offers personal benefits such as increased confidence and satisfaction. It can even lead to improved job performance, increased responsibility, and higher pay.

The Benefits of Professional Development

The benefits of professional development are many and varied, and they extend far beyond simply improving your job prospects. Some of the key benefits of professional development include:

❖   Increased knowledge and skills: Professional development enables you to learn new skills relevant to your job and improve upon existing ones.

❖   Improved job performance: When you have up-to-date knowledge and skills, you are better equipped to perform your job effectively, leading to improved performance and job satisfaction.

❖ Increased job opportunities: With new skills and knowledge, you are more competitive in the job market, increasing your chances of finding new job opportunities or advancing within your current company.

❖ Higher earning potential: Improved job performance and increased skill sets can lead to promotions and salary increases.

❖ Personal growth and satisfaction: By continuing to learn and grow, you can experience personal growth and satisfaction, leading to greater confidence and self-esteem.

How to Use this Guide

This guide is designed to be an interactive tool to help you plan and execute your professional development goals. Each chapter focuses on a different aspect of professional development and offers practical advice and exercises to help you identify your needs, set goals, and achieve success.

The Structure of the Guide

The guide is organized into 20 chapters, each focused on a different area of professional development, from assessing your needs to developing entrepreneurial skills. Each chapter offers practical tips and strategies to help you achieve your professional development goals.

Who Should Read This Guide

This guide is intended for anyone looking to enhance their career prospects, whether you're just starting out in your career, looking to advance within your current company, or seeking a new career path. It's also for those who want to remain relevant and competitive in their industry by keeping up with the latest advancements and trends.

In the next chapter, we'll explore how to assess your professional development needs, identify your goals, and create an action plan to help you achieve success.

CHAPTER 2: ASSESSING YOUR PROFESSIONAL DEVELOPMENT NEEDS

Professional development is a lifelong journey, and the first step is assessing your professional development needs. In this chapter, we will discuss how to identify your strengths and weaknesses, understand your career goals, determine your preferred learning styles, seek feedback from others, analyze areas for improvement, develop an action plan, and set clear objectives.

Identifying Your Strengths and Weaknesses

The first step in assessing your professional development needs is to identify your strengths and weaknesses. Identify what you're good at, what you can improve on, and what skills you need to develop to advance in your career. Ask yourself, what do you enjoy doing most in your current role? What tasks do you struggle with? Do you have the necessary skills to accomplish your goals? It's important to be honest with yourself during this process because it will help you understand where you need to focus your professional development efforts.

Understanding Your Career Goals

The next step in assessing your professional development needs is understanding your career goals. What do you want to achieve in your career? Do you want to become a manager? Move into a different area of your company? Change careers completely? Your goals will help you determine what skills you need to develop and what areas you need to improve on. It's important to have a clear understanding of what you want to accomplish in your career, as this will help guide your professional development efforts.

Identifying Knowledge and Skill Gaps

Identifying knowledge and skill gaps is essential in assessing your professional development needs. Look at your current role and ask yourself what knowledge and skills you need to be successful. Do you need to learn more about a particular software program or technology? Do you need to develop your leadership skills? Once you have identified your gaps, you can start to develop a plan to fill those gaps.

Determining Your Preferred Learning Styles

Everyone learns differently, so it's important to determine your preferred learning styles. Do you learn best by reading? Listening? Hands-on training? Understanding your preferred learning style will help you determine the best approach to your professional development.

Seeking Feedback From Others

Seeking feedback from others is critical in assessing your professional development needs. Ask your manager, colleagues, and mentors for feedback on your performance. Ask them what they think your strengths and weaknesses are, and what you can do to improve. Feedback is essential in identifying areas where you need to develop your skills further.

Analyzing Areas for Improvement

Once you've identified your strengths and weaknesses, career goals, knowledge and skill gaps, preferred learning styles, and received feedback from others, it's time to analyze the areas for improvement. Be specific about the areas where you need improvement and consider how you will fill those gaps. Identify any obstacles that may prevent you from reaching your goals and brainstorm ways to overcome them.

Developing an Action Plan

Developing an action plan is the next step in assessing your professional development needs. Your action plan should be specific, measurable, achievable, relevant, and time-bound. Identify the learning activities and resources you will use to develop your skills, set deadlines, and identify what success looks like. Remember to be flexible, as your professional development needs may change over time.

Setting Clear Objectives

Setting clear objectives is crucial in assessing your professional development needs. Clear objectives will guide your actions and help you measure your progress. Objectives should be aligned with your career goals and specific to the areas you need to develop. Set realistic and achievable objectives and celebrate your achievements along the way.

Final Thoughts

Assessing your professional development needs is the first step in creating a comprehensive professional development plan. By identifying your strengths and weaknesses, understanding your career goals, determining your preferred learning styles, seeking feedback from others, analyzing areas for improvement, developing an action plan, and setting clear objectives, you'll be on your way to achieving your professional development goals. Remember, professional development is a lifelong journey, and it's never too late to start.

CHAPTER 3: CREATING A PROFESSIONAL DEVELOPMENT PLAN

Professional development is a continuous process that involves enhancing your skills and knowledge to help you excel in your career. In this chapter we will focus on creating a comprehensive plan to help you achieve your professional development goals.

Developing a Comprehensive Plan

The first step in creating a professional development plan is to identify your goals and objectives. Your objectives should be specific, measurable, achievable, relevant, and time-bound. Determine what skills you need to acquire or improve and consider how these skills will help you to achieve your career goals.

Once you have identified your goals, consider how you will achieve them. List the training courses, certifications, mentorship programs, conferences, or any other educational resources that will help you achieve these goals. Consider which of these resources will be helpful for both your current job and for your future career aspirations.

It's also important to consider the potential cost of undertaking these training courses or programs. Determine whether your employer offers any financial support for career development activities. If not, consider the cost of funding your development activities out of pocket.

Identifying the Right Resources

Once you have identified your goals and the resources available to achieve them, it's time to prioritize the resources you need to invest your time and money in. Consider your goals; are there certain skills that if you acquired would be a quick win for your current job or that will help to get closer to your future goals?

Consider the different types of resources available that will help you achieve your goals. In addition to formal training courses, there are also other educational resources such as online courses, books, webinars, podcasts, and so on. Determine which ones will be most effective for your learning style.

Creating a Learning Schedule

With a clear understanding of how you will achieve your goals, create a learning schedule. When mapping out your learning schedule, factor in the time that you have available for professional development amidst your work and personal commitments. Be realistic and disciplined with yourself. Your development is an investment of time and resources and it's important to give it the priority it deserves.

Incorporating Goal Setting Strategies

In this book, we emphasize the importance of continually setting goals. With a learning schedule in hand, set small and specific milestones that will help you monitor your progress. Celebrate small wins and they will motivate you to continue putting in effort.

Structuring Your Learning Environment

One factor that can significantly impact your success in professional development is the environment in which you learn and study. Establish a dedicated study space free of any distractions. Make sure that the space is comfortable and conducive to concentrating.

Incorporating Self-Motivation Techniques

It's never easy to undertake development activities, but the rewards are always worth any challenges. To stay motivated, set yourself reminders of why you want to learn and what benefits will come from it. This keeps the end goal in sight and motivates you to persevere any challenges that may come your way.

Learning to Manage Time Effectively

Managing your time effectively is key to achieving your goals and ensuring you retain a work-life balance. Keep track of your learning schedule and manage your commitments to allow for designated learning time. Consistent and regular practice ensures you make progress towards your goals, no matter how small the progress.

Evaluating and Adjusting Your Plan

Finally, evaluate your plan. Think about what has worked and what has not worked. Consider the goals you have achieved and whether any new goals have arisen. Evaluate the effectiveness of each learning resource that you have used and whether you will continue to use it for future learning. Be flexible and adjust your plan as circumstances change.

Conclusion

Developing a comprehensive professional development plan is an important step in enhancing your career and achieving your career goals. Once you have identified your goals and the resources you require, create a learning schedule, and incorporate self-motivation techniques, goal setting strategies, and effective time management. Regularly evaluate your plan and adapt it when needed, because the surest way to achieve your goals is through taking consistent and thoughtful action towards them.

CHAPTER 4: BUILDING YOUR PROFESSIONAL NETWORK

As the saying goes, it's not what you know, it's who you know. Networking is crucial to building a successful career and is a vital part of professional development. In this chapter, we will explore the importance of networking, how to build professional relationships, attending professional conferences and events, joining professional organizations, participating in online communities, finding a mentor or coach, building your personal brand, and leveraging your network for success.

Understanding the Importance of Networking

Networking is all about building relationships with people in your industry or related fields, with the understanding that this is a two-way street. You offer your knowledge, expertise, or assistance, and in return, you can tap into their experience, ideas, and connections. Networking is not just about attending events or meeting people for the first time, but it's about building long-lasting professional relationships. A strong network can help with job opportunities, career advancement, personal development, and can lead to a fulfilling professional life.

Building Professional Relationships

Building relationships in a professional setting requires time and effort. You should focus on building authentic relationships rather than just seeking opportunities. Here are some tips to build lasting professional relationships:

❖ Be Authentic: Networking is about people, so it's essential to be yourself and make genuine connections based on shared values or interests.

❖ Listen: Listen attentively to what others have to say. This permits you to develop an understanding and build empathy among peers.

❖ Be Helpful: Offer help or support whenever you can, and make sure to follow up appropriately to show that you are reliable and committed.

❖ Follow-Up: Keep in touch regularly after you met people, regularly share your insights with them.

❖ Be Memorable: Leave a lasting impression by sharing your unique strengths, like a talent or skill that others can remember and mention specifically.

Attending Professional Conferences and Events

Attending conferences, symposiums, and other industry-related events, can be a great way to meet other professionals in your industry face-to-face. Conferences provide an opportunity for personal development, networking, and learning about new advancements in your field. Once there, make sure to interact with other attendees, ask questions about their experience or industry-related topics, and make a point to connect with them after the conference through social media or email.

Joining Professional Organizations

Joining a professional organization can be a great way to get involved in your industry and expand your network. Professional organizations can provide access to knowledge, resources, and opportunities, as well as provide a forum for discussions and sharing experiences. You can have access to the latest information or technology trends and participate in training and development programs.

Participating in Online Communities

The use and benefit of social media are not limited to casual interactions. Social media and discussion groups are an excellent way to expand your network to people who might be outside your geographic region. Joining these groups allows you to engage in online discussions, share your opinions, and learn from senior professionals.

Finding a Mentor or Coach

A mentor can provide guidance and advice throughout your career, while a coach can help you to focus specifically on personal development. These experienced professionals can offer valuable insights, help you set goals, provide feedback, and challenge you in ways that will inspire growth in your career.

Building Your Personal Brand

Whether you are an entrepreneur or employed, it is crucial to establish your personal brand. Your personal brand represents who you are as a professional. Your personal brand should reflect your strengths as well as your unique value proposition. Focus on projecting confidence and capabilities in all of your interactions and be sure to keep your professional social media profiles updated to tell your story effectively.

Leveraging Your Network for Success

Once you have established a strong network, it's essential to learn how to leverage it effectively. Always make sure to nurture existing relationships and make new connections whenever possible. Make a point to assist others in your network whenever they need support. Keep your network engaged by sharing industry insights or information that they might find valuable. Be genuine and direct when seeking assistance or guidance, being mindful of how you can reciprocate in the future.

Conclusion

Building your professional network can be a highly effective way to advance your career. Networking provides access to valuable expertise, resources, and job opportunities, but requires effort to build and maintain strong relationships. Understanding the importance of networking, participating in industry events, and joining professional communities can all be effective ways of expanding and nurturing your professional network. By investing time and energy into building your network, you can establish lifelong relationships and take your career to the next level.

CHAPTER 5: DEVELOPING LEADERSHIP SKILLS

Leadership is the ability to inspire, guide, and motivate others towards a common goal or vision. It involves qualities such as strong communication skills, the ability to delegate effectively, developing a strong team, and making decisions that drive positive results. In today's fast-paced and constantly evolving business environment, developing strong leadership skills is crucial for career success. This chapter outlines some key practices to help professionals to become effective and inspiring leaders.

Understanding the Qualities of a Good Leader

Being a good leader involves having a combination of both soft and hard skills. Soft skills include qualities such as effective communication, empathy, and emotional intelligence. Hard skills, on the other hand, refer to technical skills and knowledge. An inspiring leader also acknowledges the importance of serving as a role model for their team, taking responsibility for their own actions, and demonstrating the values and behaviours they expect from their team members.

Developing Effective Communication Skills

Effective communication is a key aspect of leadership. Leaders must be able to communicate clearly and effectively with team members, clients, and stakeholders. They need to be able to articulate goals, expectations, and instructions clearly, and to listen carefully to feedback from team members and others. To master effective communication, developing strong presentation skills can be an important tool. This involves taking time to prepare well, developing compelling content and making use of effective visual aids.

Learning to Delegate Effectively

Delegation is a core leadership skill which involves assigning tasks and responsibilities to team members to build confidence and demonstrate trust. Successful delegation involves identifying the right tasks for each team member based on their strengths and weaknesses, and providing clear instructions to ensure the task is completed on time and meets required standards. Leaders need to be able to strike the right balance, delegating enough to stimulate growth of team members, but not so much that they become overwhelmed, or the overall quality of work declines.

Building a Strong Team

A strong team can achieve incredible results. Building an effective team requires developing a team based culture that supports growth, collaboration, and innovation. Leaders need to understand the importance of hiring the right people for the right roles and fostering an environment which helps team members to learn from one another. Encouraging team members to share ideas, knowledge, and experiences can also enhance their growth and innovation potential.

Motivating and Inspiring Others

Motivation and inspiration are key ingredients in leadership.

Leaders need to be able to inspire team members to achieve great results. Motivation involves understanding each team member's individual drivers - what motivates them, and what truly drives them to excel. Leaders need to be able to communicate a clear vision for their team, identify each team member's contribution to the shared vision, and provide timely feedback to reinforce the positives. Leaders must also be prepared to exhibit a growth mindset, committing to their own learning and growth development.

Making Decisions and Solving Problems

Successful leaders must be able to make timely and informed decisions. They also need to be able to solve problems quickly and efficiently. One good approach to solving problems is the 5 Whys Method, which involves asking a series of questions to identify the root cause of a problem. Leaders also need to be prepared to take calculated risks and make difficult decisions, having the courage and conviction to see them through to successful resolution.

Managing Conflict and Confrontation

Effective leaders also need to possess conflict resolution skills. Conflict is an inevitable part of the workplace, and unless handled effectively, it can escalate and impact productivity negatively. Leaders need to be able to remain calm under pressure, listen actively, and remain objective. Doing so allows leaders to find common ground and a pathway forward that benefits everyone.

Developing Emotional Intelligence

Emotional intelligence refers to the ability to recognize, understand, and manage one's own emotions as well as the emotions of others. Leaders with high emotional intelligence are better equipped at building positive relationships, inspiring team members, and managing difficult situations positively. Emotional intelligence involves developing empathy and remaining self-aware in diverse circumstances, and ultimately enabling individuals to make thoughtful, considered input into a team's culture, communication, and development.

In conclusion, developing effective leadership skills is crucial for career success. Leaders need to possess qualities such as strong communication skills, the ability to delegate effectively, strong team building skills, and the courage to make tough decisions. Leaders also need to develop emotional intelligence, the ability to remain calm under pressure, and the ability to manage conflict effectively. Invoking these qualities can lead to success in leadership roles and ultimately to drive value for an organization.

CHAPTER 6: ENHANCING YOUR TECHNICAL SKILLS

In today's rapidly evolving technological landscape, professional development and the acquisition of new technical skills have become an essential aspect of career success. Whether we work in IT, marketing, finance, or any other industry, staying up to date with technological changes and mastering new software and applications is essential to our job performance. In this chapter, we will discuss how to enhance your technical skills for better career advancement.

Keeping Up with Technological Changes

The first step to enhancing your technical skills is to keep up with the latest technological changes and advancements. This means staying informed about the latest trends, reading relevant industry publications, and attending conferences and events. It is crucial to create a learning environment where you can acquire new knowledge through books, videos, and podcasts.

Choosing the Right Technical Tools

Once you understand the latest technological changes, you should choose the right technical tools for your job. This means selecting tools that are best suited to your work needs and goals. Suppose you work in marketing, for instance. In that case, you might need to learn about social media management tools, digital marketing software applications or Search Engine Optimization (SEO) to help you achieve your professional objectives.

Learning to Use New Software and Applications

Once you have selected the right technical tools for your job, the next step is to learn how to use them. The best way to learn is through hands-on practice and experimentation. You may desire to take a course, read the user manual, or take advantage of online tutorials or video training. Practice with the tools for some time until you become confident using them to deliver on your goals.

Expanding Your Knowledge of Cloud Computing

Cloud computing represents one of the profoundest technological shifts in the last decade. With cloud computing, you can store and process data on remote servers instead of on-premise hard drives. As such, professionals who wish to stay ahead of the curve should try to expand their knowledge of cloud computing. You should learn about cloud computing platforms like Microsoft Azure, Google Cloud Platform, and AWS. By doing so, you'll be prepared to leverage the cloud for your business processes, data storage, and other business goals.

Developing Your Coding Skills

One of the most valuable skills you can learn is coding. Coding involves writing instructions that a computer can follow. It is the building block of software and applications. If you want to enhance your technical skills, you should develop your coding skills. Programming languages like HTML, CSS, and JavaScript are excellent places to start. You can also learn Python, C++, Ruby, and other We-based development languages, depending on your job requirements.

Designing and Creating Effective Websites

In today's digital age, websites are an essential element for businesses that wish to connect with their customers and drive sales. As such, web-design skills have become increasingly significant. Designing a website requires skills in areas like user interface (UI), user experience (UX), graphic design, typography, and front-end development. Fortunately, with the abundance of online resources available, you can learn to design a website-specific to your business or professional goals.

Learning to Use Social Media Effectively

Social media platforms like Twitter, Facebook, Instagram, and LinkedIn have become critical channels through which businesses connect with their customers. Consequently, professionals who understand how to use social media platforms to engage their audience have an advantage. Developing relevant social media skills will enable you to create and implement successful social media campaigns that drive engagement, conversion, and customer loyalty for your enterprise.

Understanding Cybersecurity and Privacy Issues

With the growth of the internet, the significance of cybersecurity and privacy concerns has become increasingly important. Cybercriminals are continually developing new ways to hack software systems and steal information. Therefore, it is essential to understand important cybersecurity measures like password hygiene, two-factor authentication, and virtual private networks (VPNs), among others. Protecting your computer, mobile device, or website is critical to ensuring your professional success.

Conclusion

Enhancing your technical skills can be a challenging yet

rewarding journey. It requires hard work, dedication, and a lot of practice. However, by keeping up with technological changes, utilizing the right technical tools, learning to code, mastering social media platforms, and understanding cybersecurity and privacy concerns, you can achieve your professional goals. Remember, in today's digital age, where technology is critical to business success, every step you take towards enhancing your technical skills counts.

CHAPTER 7: IMPROVING YOUR SOFT SKILLS

Many people believe that professional success is solely based on their technical or hard skills such as coding, project management, or financial management. However, developing soft skills such as communication, interpersonal skills, emotional intelligence, time management, critical thinking, and creativity is also essential for professional growth. Soft skills can put you ahead in your career, make you more aware of your work environment and help you build meaningful relationships with your colleagues. In this chapter, we will explore some of the most important soft skills that you should develop to improve your professional development journey.

Understanding the Importance of Soft Skills

Soft skills, also known as people or interpersonal skills, are the set of personal attributes that enable you to interact effectively and harmoniously with others in the workplace. Soft skills are essential, regardless of your job or industry, and can help you stand out in a competitive job market.

Employers look for candidates with a combination of hard and soft skills. While hard skills are necessary to perform specific tasks, they can be learned on the job or through formal education. Soft skills, however, are not intuitive and require time, effort, and patience to develop.

Developing Strong Communication Skills

Effective communication is one of the most critical soft skills you should strive to develop. In the workplace, effective communication facilitates collaboration, helps avoid conflicts, and ensures that everyone is on the same page. Here are some tips to help you develop strong communication skills:

- ❖ Active Listening: Listening is vital to effective communication. Avoid interrupting the speaker, maintain eye contact, and provide feedback through verbal cues or body language.

- ❖ Clarity and Brevity: Deliver your message with clarity and conciseness. Long-winded speeches can bore or confuse the listener.

- ❖ Tailoring Your Communication: Different audiences require different communication styles. Learn to recognize who you're communicating with and tailor your message to meet their needs.

- ❖ Developing Written Communication: Develop your writing skills, as it is a critical mode of communication in any professional setting. Learn to write concise, informative and grammatically correct emails, memos, and reports.

Enhancing Your Interpersonal Skills

Interpersonal skills are the traits and behaviors that enable you to interact effectively with others. Developing interpersonal skills is essential for building and maintaining relationships in the workplace. Here are some ways you can enhance your interpersonal skills:

- ❖ Empathy: To understand and relate to others, you should

develop empathy. Empathy allows you to view situations from another person's perspective, which can help you respond more effectively.

❖   Positive Attitude: A positive attitude can make a big difference in how you interact with others. Always try to maintain a positive outlook, be approachable, and remember to smile.

❖   Conflict Resolution: Conflicts can arise in any workplace, and you should be equipped with the skills to resolve them. Learn to identify the causes of conflicts, diffuse emotions, and find win-win solutions.

❖   Collaboration: Collaboration involves working with others to achieve a shared goal. You should learn to respect other people's opinions and be willing to work with them to achieve common goals.

Building Effective Relationships

Building strong relationships with your colleagues is one of the most valuable skills you can acquire in your professional life. Building positive work relationships can lead to a more fulfilling work experience, higher job satisfaction, and better career opportunities. Here are some tips on how to build effective work relationships:

❖   Networking: Networking involves building relationships with people in your field, outside your company. Attend professional conferences, join professional organizations, or participate in online communities.

❖   Be Genuine: Be who you are. Being genuine means that you're honest about your strengths and weaknesses, which can build trust and respect.

❖   Be Respectful: Treat your colleagues with respect and

courtesy, even if you disagree with them. Avoid being overly confrontational or dismissive of others' feelings and opinions.

❖ Give Feedback: Providing constructive feedback can help build stronger relationships with your colleagues. Feedback can help people identify areas they need to improve on and feel appreciated.

Developing Your Emotional Intelligence

Emotional intelligence is the ability to identify, understand, and manage emotions in oneself and others. It involves the ability to recognize your emotions, understand their effects, and regulate your behavior accordingly. Here are some ways you can develop your emotional intelligence:

❖ Self-Awareness: Self-awareness involves understanding your emotions, beliefs, and values. It also requires acknowledging your strengths and weaknesses.

❖ Self-Management: Self-management involves regulating your emotions effectively, controlling them instead of letting them control you. Learn to direct your emotions into positive actions.

❖ Social Awareness: Social awareness involves recognizing and understanding others' emotions and being able to empathize with them.

❖ Relationship Management: Relationship management involves using your emotions to build positive relationships with others. Learn to be an effective communicator, develop conflict resolution skills, and be a good team player.

Improving Your Time Management Skills

Time management is the ability to plan and organize how

much time you spend on various tasks effectively. Effective time management skills are essential for accomplishing your goals and objectives. Here are some tips for improving your time management skills:

❖ Setting Priorities: Identify what tasks are most important and prioritize them accordingly.

❖ Making a Schedule: Create a schedule and stick to it. Be sure to include adequate time for work, breaks, and leisure activities.

❖ Avoiding Procrastination: Don't delay or postpone tasks. Try to tackle them as soon as possible and avoid distractions such as social media or unnecessary meetings.

❖ Learning to Say No: Saying no can be difficult, but it's essential to manage your time effectively. Be realistic about what you can accomplish and say no to tasks that aren't a priority.

Developing Critical Thinking and Problem-Solving Skills

Critical thinking is the ability to analyze and evaluate information objectively and to make reasoned judgments. Problem-solving involves coming up with solutions to issues or obstacles. Developing these skills requires practice, but it's essential for professional development. Here are some ways you can develop your critical thinking and problem-solving skills:

1. Analyzing Information: Develop your analytical skills by evaluating information critically. Examine assumptions and look for inconsistencies.

2. Creativity: Creativity involves coming up with new ideas and thinking outside the box. Look for ways to approach problems differently and challenge conventional thinking.

3. Decision Making: Decision-making is the process of choosing

the best course of action from among several options. Consider the available options and the consequences of each before making a decision.

4. Problem Solving: Problem-solving involves identifying problems, brainstorming solutions, and putting them into action. Be creative and persistent in developing and implementing solutions.

Enhancing Your Creativity

Creativity is the ability to come up with new ideas and concepts or to see things in a different way. Developing your creativity can help you be more innovative, productive and find solutions to problems. Here are some tips for enhancing your creativity:

- ❖ Brainstorming: Brainstorming is a technique that involves generating a large number of ideas quickly and without judgment. Encourage others to contribute ideas by hosting brainstorming sessions.

- ❖ Combining Ideas: Combining unrelated ideas can lead to new and innovative ideas. Look for ways to combine disparate ideas to generate new solutions.

- ❖ Creative Environment: Creating a physical and psychological environment that fosters creativity can help you be more creative. Surround yourself with objects that inspire you and take breaks to recharge your creative energy.

- ❖ Taking Risks: Take calculated risks by stepping out of your comfort zone. Experiment with new approaches or strategies, and don't let fear of failure stop you from taking risks.

Conclusion

Soft skills significantly impact your professional development and career growth. The skills mentioned above are fundamental and require continuous practice and improvement. Invest time in self-growth to improve these skills continuously. Developing these skills will help you work collaboratively in a team, communicate more effectively, and solve problems creatively. Remember, learning is an ongoing process, and professional development is one of the keys to achieving your career goals.

CHAPTER 8:
MASTERING PROJECT MANAGEMENT

If you work in any industry that involves delivering products or services, you will likely have been involved in some sort of project management. Whether your team is building a new website, developing a new product, or planning an event, project management skills are essential to ensuring projects stay on track and deliver the desired outcomes. In this chapter, we will delve deeper into the principles of project management and provide you with the tools and techniques necessary to master it.

Understanding the Principles of Project Management

Project management is the practice of planning, executing, and closing out a project. With project management, you aim to deliver a product or service within a defined scope, budget, and timeline. The practice involves balancing competing demands on resources, such as time, cost, scope, and quality. Project management is used in virtually every industry, from construction to software development to health care.

Developing a Project Plan

To successfully manage a project, you need to start by developing a project plan. A project plan defines the scope of the project, the goals and objectives you aim to achieve, the timelines, milestones, budget, and available resources.

Defining Project Scope and Objectives

The project scope outlines the parameters of the project and defines what the project will and will not achieve. To define the project scope effectively, you need to have a clear understanding of the project objectives. The objectives should be measurable in terms of the desired outcomes and should be aligned with the overall goals of the organization.

Developing a Project Timeline

Once you have defined the project scope and objectives, you need to develop a project timeline. The timeline should include all the key activities required to complete the project, including deadlines and milestones. You should also consider the dependencies between activities to ensure that the project stays on track.

Allocating Resources and Budgets

Another critical aspect of project management is resource allocation. You need to ensure that you have enough resources, such as people, money, and materials, to deliver the project effectively. You also need to ensure that you allocate resources based on the project priorities and budget constraints.

Managing Project Risks

Projects are inherently risky endeavors, and managing risks is a critical aspect of project management. You need to identify potential risks, assess their likelihood and impact, and develop strategies to mitigate them. Project risks can include anything from changes in the project scope to resource constraints to unforeseen external events that can impact the project.

Monitoring Progress and Making Adjustments

Finally, project management involves monitoring progress and making adjustments, as necessary. You need to track project performance against the project plan, identify variances, and take corrective action, as necessary. This involves monitoring progress against the project timeline, tracking budget and resources, and ensuring that the project is meeting the desired outcomes.

Closing out Projects Successfully

At the end of a project, you need to close it out effectively. This involves ensuring that all deliverables have been completed, that the project has met the desired outcomes, and that any outstanding issues have been addressed. Additionally, you should conduct a project post-mortem to review the project's successes and failures and identify areas for future improvement.

Project management is an essential skill for any professional. By mastering project management, you can ensure that your projects stay on track, meet the desired outcomes, and deliver value for your organization.

CHAPTER 9: IMPROVING CUSTOMER SERVICE AND SATISFACTION

In today's competitive business landscape, customer service is one of the most essential elements of success. The quality of service that customers receive can make or break a business. Therefore, it is crucial for all professionals to understand the importance of creating a customer-centric approach, improving customer experience, and enhancing customer satisfaction. This chapter will discuss the key strategies that professionals can use to improve customer service and satisfaction.

Understanding the Importance of Customer Service

An integral part of professional development is learning to understand the importance of customer service. Customer service is the act of providing support to customers before, during, and after a purchase. It involves providing assistance, resolving issues, and communicating with customers. Customers expect top-notch service, and businesses that make it a priority to exceed their expectations are often more successful in the long run. By providing excellent customer service, companies can enhance customer loyalty, increase revenues and profits, and build a positive reputation.

Developing Strong Communication Skills

Effective customer service starts with strong communication skills. Professionals must be able to communicate with customers, listen actively, and respond to their needs. They should be able to communicate clearly, professionally, and empathetically. Understanding the customer's point of view is essential to providing the best possible service. It is important to avoid using technical jargon and adapt communication to the customer's level of understanding.

Building Effective Relationships with Customers

Building strong relationships with customers is critical to creating a positive customer service experience. Professionals must engage with customers, make them feel welcome, and go the extra mile to satisfy their needs. They should be friendly and approachable, and they should take the time to understand customer concerns. By building a good relationship with customers, they will be more likely to return and recommend the business to others.

Handling Difficult Customers and Situations

Every business encounters difficult customers and situations from time to time. For professionals, managing difficult customers can be one of the most challenging aspects of customer service. Professionals must be able to handle stressful situations, remain calm and composed, and find solutions that are beneficial to both the customer and the business. They should listen to the customer's concerns and try to understand their point of view. By being empathetic, responsive, and maintaining a positive attitude, professionals can effectively manage difficult customers and situations.

Managing Customer Service Expectations

Managing customer service expectations is a critical factor in providing excellent service to customers. Professionals should set clear expectations for what customers can expect in terms of service, response times, and outcomes. They should also provide accurate information about products and services, pricing, and delivery timeframes. By managing customer expectations, businesses can enhance trust and loyalty, and minimize the likelihood of negative reviews or complaints.

Developing Effective Conflict Resolution Skills

Resolving conflicts is an essential skill that all professionals should possess. Conflicts can arise with customers or colleagues, and it's crucial to create a positive outcome. Professionals must have problem-solving skills, interpret situations, and understand both parties' viewpoints. It's essential to remain calm and maintain the customer's trust while finding a compromise. By mastering conflict resolution skills, professionals can create a positive outcome and minimize damage to the business's reputation.

Using Data and Analytics to Improve Customer Service

Data and analytics can provide valuable insights into customer behavior, preferences, and expectations. Professionals should use this data to improve customer service and satisfaction. By analyzing customer data, companies can create a personalized experience for each customer, which can lead to more positive outcomes. By understanding customer interactions, professionals can recognize potential issues before they arise, enabling proactive measures to improve customer satisfaction.

Developing Customer Service Metrics and KPIs

Key performance indicators (KPIs) and metrics can be a significant source of information for businesses seeking to improve customer service. KPIs track and measure progress toward a set of specific and measurable goals. By using KPIs and metrics, professionals can gain insights into how effectively they're serving customers and areas where they can improve. They can use metrics to measure customer satisfaction, retention rates, and overall customer experience. This information can then be used to develop strategies for improving customer service in the future.

Conclusion

Improving customer service and satisfaction is a critical component of professional development. By understanding the importance of customer service, developing strong communication skills, building effective relationships with customers, managing customer expectations, and mastering conflict resolution skills, professionals can provide top-notch service to their customers. By using data and analytics, tracking KPIs and metrics, they can continuously monitor and improve customer service levels. By creating positive customer experiences, professionals can enhance their company's reputation, build customer loyalty, increase revenues, and set themselves apart from the competition.

CHAPTER 10: LEARNING TO INNOVATE

Innovation is defined as the process of creating something new or improving an existing product or service. It is crucial for businesses to innovate in order to stay ahead of the competition and meet the ever-changing needs and wants of customers. In this chapter, we will cover the importance of innovation and how to develop a culture of innovation within your organization.

Understanding the Importance of Innovation

Innovation is vital for the growth and success of any business. It can help you stay ahead of the competition, increase revenue, reduce costs, improve products or services, and drive customer satisfaction. Innovative companies are known for being adaptable, resilient, and able to anticipate and respond to changes in the market.

Learning to Think Outside the Box

One of the keys to being innovative is to learn to think outside the box. This means challenging assumptions, exploring new possibilities, and approaching problems from different angles. It involves taking risks, being open to new and unconventional ideas, and not being afraid of failure. Embracing failure as a learning opportunity can help foster a culture of innovation within your organization.

Encouraging Creative Thinking in Your Team

Innovation is not just the responsibility of a single person or department; it requires the input and collaboration of everyone within the organization. Encouraging creative thinking in your team can lead to groundbreaking ideas and unique solutions. Providing opportunities for brainstorming sessions, cross-functional projects, and diversity of thought can help spark creativity and innovation.

Creating an Innovative Culture

An innovative culture is one that fosters and rewards creativity, risk-taking, and experimentation. It involves encouraging employees to share their ideas, providing the necessary resources and tools to develop and test those ideas, and providing support and recognition for successful innovation. Creating a culture of innovation starts with top leadership and a commitment to creating an environment where innovation is encouraged and celebrated.

Managing the Innovation Process

Innovation is not just about generating ideas; it also involves managing the innovation process effectively. This includes prioritizing and testing ideas, developing a strategy for implementation, and tracking and measuring the success of innovation initiatives. It requires a balance of creativity and discipline to ensure that innovative ideas are not only generated but also implemented successfully.

Testing and Refining Ideas

Testing and refining innovative ideas is a crucial step in the innovation process. A prototype or pilot program can help identify any potential issues or challenges before a full-scale implementation. It can also provide valuable feedback from customers and stakeholders that can be used to improve the product or service. Testing and refining should be an iterative process, where feedback is continuously incorporated to improve the final product.

Bringing Ideas to Market

Bringing innovative ideas to market involves developing a go-to-market strategy that includes pricing, distribution, and marketing tactics. It requires a deep understanding of the target customer, market trends, and competitive landscape. Successful innovation involves not only creating a unique product or service but also effectively communicating its value proposition to customers.

Measuring Innovation Success

Measuring the success of innovation initiatives involves identifying key performance indicators (KPIs) and tracking progress against those KPIs. Metrics such as customer satisfaction rates, revenue growth, and market share can provide valuable insights into the impact of innovation on your business. Regularly reviewing and analyzing these metrics can help identify areas of improvement and ensure that your innovation initiatives are aligned with your overall business strategy.

Conclusion

Innovation is a crucial element of professional development, and it requires a culture of creativity, risk-taking, and collaboration. Stay ahead of the competition and meet the ever-changing needs and wants of customers by learning to think outside the box, encouraging creative thinking in your team, creating an innovative culture, managing the innovation process effectively, testing and refining ideas, bringing ideas to market, and measuring innovation success. Remember, innovation is not a one-time effort, it requires continual learning, adaptation, and the ability to embrace failure as a learning opportunity.

CHAPTER 11: IMPROVING YOUR PRESENTATION SKILLS

Presentation skills are essential when it comes to effective communication in the workplace. Whether you are presenting to a small group of colleagues or a large group of senior management, it's crucial to deliver your message with confidence and clarity. However, many people struggle with public speaking and presentations, and this can hinder their professional growth and their ability to succeed in their roles. In this chapter, we explore techniques that can help to improve your presentation skills.

Understanding the Importance of Effective Presentations

Firstly, it's essential to understand why effective presentations are so crucial in the workplace. In many cases, your presentation may be the only opportunity to influence your audience's thoughts or decisions. An effective presentation can persuade others to take action, whether it's to buy a product, invest in a project or support a new initiative. Effective presentations can also help to build connections, expand your network and increase your visibility within your organization.

Developing Your Public Speaking Skills

Effective public speaking skills are fundamental to delivering an effective presentation. Many people feel nervous before public speaking, but with practice, you can develop the confidence to deliver presentations with ease. Start by finding opportunities to speak in front of people, such as volunteering to present at team meetings or speaking at local events. It's also essential to understand your audience and their needs. Tailor your message to meet their requirements and speak in a tone and language that they can relate to.

Understanding Your Audience

One of the key factors in delivering an effective presentation is understanding and engaging your audience. Before you begin, take the time to research your audience and determine their needs, interests and expectations. Consider their level of knowledge on the subject, their age, gender, cultural background and learning preferences. This information will allow you to personalize your presentation and ensure that your message resonates with your audience.

Developing Compelling Content

A critical aspect of presenting is the content of your speech. Ensure that it is well-structured, clear, concise, and contains value. The format might include a captivating introduction, clear points of discussion, timed breaks, and a persuasive call to action to finish. Determine what you aim to achieve with the presentation, and then, create a structure to ensure that you stay on track and that your message is heard loud and clear.

Creating Effective Visual Aids

Visual aids such as slides, charts, and graphics can aid in delivering an effective presentation as they serve as tools to emphasize and elaborate on your message. However, it's important to limit the number of visual aids used in a presentation and ensure that they complement your message rather than detract from it. Focus on simplicity and clarity and use strong visuals to support your key messages.

Practicing and Rehearsing Your Presentation

Once you've developed your content and visual aids, it's essential to practice your presentation. Public speaking is a skill, and like any other skill, it requires practice to improve. Practice your presentation in front of a mirror, with friends or colleagues or even record yourself on video to assess how you sound and your delivery. Rehearse until you feel confident and comfortable with your presentation, and you can deliver it without relying heavily on notes.

Engaging Your Audience

Finally, it's crucial to engage your audience throughout your presentation to keep them interested and attentive. Use anecdotes, humor, or examples to illustrate your points where relevant. Encourage audience participation, for example, by asking questions, seeking feedback, and creating opportunities for group discussions or interactive sessions. Remember to speak clearly and at an appropriate pace and maintain eye contact with your audience.

Handling Questions and Feedback

After delivering your presentation, expect some questions and feedback from your audience. Learn how to handle these interactions with confidence. Be prepared to answer their questions and to receive feedback, whether positive or negative, gracefully. If you cannot answer a question, have a response on how you would find the answer or promise to follow up with the answer via email soon after your presentation. Remember to thank your audience for their time and attention.

Conclusion

In conclusion, delivering effective presentations can help you grow personally and professionally. By focusing on your public speaking skills, understanding your audience, developing compelling content and visual aids, practicing and rehearsing, engaging your audience, and handling feedback confidently, you can deliver presentations with ease. Use these techniques to help improve your presentation skills and become a more effective communicator in the workplace.

CHAPTER 12: CULTIVATING EMOTIONAL INTELLIGENCE

Emotional intelligence refers to the ability to recognize and manage your own emotions, while also being able to empathize with others' emotions and respond appropriately in various situations. Developing emotional intelligence can have a significant impact on your personal and professional life. In this chapter, we will explore the importance of emotional intelligence and provide practical tips to cultivate it.

Understanding the Importance of Emotional Intelligence

In today's fast-paced business environment, emotional intelligence is becoming an increasingly important skill for professionals to possess. Studies have shown that individuals with high emotional intelligence are more likely to be successful in their careers, have stronger relationships, and better mental health.

When we have a high level of emotional intelligence, we are able to manage our own emotions, which can help us stay calm in stressful situations, think more clearly, and make better decisions. Additionally, emotional intelligence allows us to understand

and empathize with others' emotions, which can lead to more effective communication, stronger relationships, and better team dynamics.

Developing Self-Awareness

The first step in cultivating emotional intelligence is to develop self-awareness. This involves being able to recognize and understand your own emotions. One way to do this is to take time to reflect on your feelings and understand what triggers them. When you are able to identify your emotions, you can learn to manage them in a healthy and effective way.

Understanding Your Emotions and Triggers

To develop self-awareness, it is important to understand your emotions and what triggers them. Start by noticing how you feel in different situations and try to identify the specific emotions you are experiencing. For example, you may find that you feel anxious when you receive an urgent email from your boss or angry when a coworker takes credit for your work.

Once you have identified your emotions, take time to reflect on what triggers them. Are there specific situations that always make you feel a certain way? Are there certain people or behaviors that trigger a negative reaction?

Developing Empathy for Others

Empathy is the ability to understand and share the feelings of others. To cultivate empathy, it is important to practice active listening and pay attention to nonverbal cues. When someone is speaking to you, try to focus on what they are saying and how they are saying it. Pay attention to their tone of voice, facial expressions, and body language to get a better understanding of their emotions.

Building Strong Relationships

Building strong relationships is a key component of emotional intelligence. When we have strong relationships with others, we are better able to understand and empathize with their emotions. This can help us communicate more effectively and build stronger teams.

To build strong relationships, it is important to communicate openly and honestly. Be willing to listen to others and try to understand their perspectives. Show appreciation for others and recognize their contributions.

Managing Emotions in Difficult Situations

In difficult situations, it can be challenging to manage our emotions. However, when we are able to stay calm and rational, we are better able to find solutions to problems and avoid making impulsive decisions.

One way to manage emotions in difficult situations is to take a step back and take a deep breath. This can help you calm down and refocus your thoughts. It is also helpful to remember that you have the power to control your reactions. Instead of reacting impulsively, take time to reflect and respond in a thoughtful and measured way.

Developing Conflict Resolution Skills

Conflict is a natural part of any workplace. To effectively manage conflict, it is important to develop strong conflict resolution skills. This involves being able to communicate effectively, listen actively, and find mutually beneficial solutions.

When faced with conflict, try to remain calm and focused. Avoid using accusatory language and instead focus on using "I" statements to express your perspective. Show empathy for the other person's point of view and work to find a solution that benefits everyone involved.

Managing Stress and Burnout

Finally, it is important to develop strategies to manage stress and avoid burnout. When we are overwhelmed and stressed, it can be challenging to manage our emotions effectively. To avoid burnout, make sure to take time for self-care, such as exercise, meditation, or spending time with friends and family. Set boundaries around work and prioritize your time to ensure that you are able to manage your workload effectively.

In conclusion, emotional intelligence is a key skill for professionals to develop in order to be successful in their careers and personal lives. To cultivate emotional intelligence, it is important to develop self-awareness, empathy, strong relationships, conflict resolution skills, and strategies to manage stress and burnout. By developing these skills, you can improve your communication, build stronger teams, and become a more effective leader.

CHAPTER 13: ENHANCING YOUR CREATIVITY

As the world continues to merge, individuals are expected to possess a broader range of skills, including creativity. In this digital age where automation is threatening jobs in various fields, creativity has become even more valuable because machines cannot replace it. However, not everyone considers themselves creative, and the pressure to be creative can cause some people to feel overwhelmed.

Creativity is essential to pushing forward new ideas, improving existing processes, and developing innovative solutions. This chapter explores the creative process and discusses how individuals can develop their creativity through various techniques.

Understanding The Creative Process

Creativity is the ability to create something new or imaginative. The creative process is extensive, varying from person to person, but it involves four significant stages:

❖ Preparation: This stage involves research, gathering resources, and finding inspiration or motivation. It is about collecting the raw materials needed to start work.

❖ Incubation: This stage is about letting the collected

information sink in. During this time, the mind is subconsciously processing all the data gathered in the preparation stage to create new ideas.

❖ Illumination: This is the "Aha!" moment when the idea comes to mind. The idea is clear, and it feels like a revelation.

❖ Execution: This is the process of turning the idea into reality. This is where the creative process becomes intentional, and the project is brought to life.

Developing A Creative Mindset

A creative mindset is achievable by anyone. It means that one can approach anything with an open mind and see it from different perspectives. Here are some tips for developing a creative mindset:

❖ Embrace Your Experiences - Every experience has the potential to inspire creativity. Experiences can include conversations, travel, work, or personal setbacks. Every experience is unique, and it can be used to inspire new ideas.

❖ Start With A Beginner's Mind - This means approaching every project with a fresh perspective. Letting go of preconceived ideas or assumptions can open new ways to approach problems.

❖ Build Your Mental Filters - Mental filters are ways in which people selectively interpret information. Building mental filters can help to focus on the information that is important to a project.

Building A Creative Environment

Creating an environment that promotes creativity is essential. Here are some tips to make an environment where creativity can flourish:

❖ Create An Open And Safe Environment - Fostering an open and safe environment encourages individuals to share their ideas without fear of criticism or rejection. It is essential to listen to every idea without judgment.

❖ Remove Barriers To Creativity - Barriers such as the fear of failure, perfectionism, or being too self-critical can hinder creativity. Try to remove these barriers and remain open to different perspectives and solutions.

❖ Stimulate Creativity - Choose colors, decor, lighting, music, and even furniture that stimulate creativity. Use a range of sensory cues, such as scent and touch, too.

Learning To Brainstorm Effectively

Brainstorming is the process by which individuals or teams generate ideas in a free-form manner. Here are some tips to make a brainstorming session more effective:

❖ Remove Distractions - Turn off distractions such as mobile phones and other electronics. Assign one person to be a scribe or use an online tool, to document the ideas.

❖ Foster A Non-Judgmental Environment - Brainstorming sessions should be free of criticism, evaluation, or judgment. It is essential to let the ideas flow freely, without fear or hesitation.

❖ Start With A Clear Question - A clear directive or question can help to focus the brainstorming session. It is essential to choose a well-defined question or problem, so the session does not stray off-course.

Using Innovation Tools And Techniques

Innovation tools and techniques are methods that can promote creativity and bring ideas to life. Here are some useful tools for stimulating creativity:

❖ Mind Maps - Mind maps are diagrams used to connect ideas or concepts visually. They allow individuals to think more freely, quickly, and creatively.

❖ SCAMPER Technique - This is an acronym for Substitute, Combine, Adapt, Modify, Put to Another Use, Eliminate, and Reverse/Rearrange. It is a technique used to create new ideas from existing ones.

❖ Analogical Thinking - This involves drawing comparisons between things that are seemingly not related. Analogical thinking can spur creativity and help to discover unique approaches to problems.

Collaborating On Creative Projects

Collaboration is a central tenet of creativity. Joining forces with like-minded individuals can lead to creative solutions. Here are some tips to make collaboration more effective:

❖ Identify Roles - Identify the roles that need to be filled. Each person's skills and talents should complement each other.

❖ Ensure Open Communication - Communication is key to collaboration. It is essential to set clear expectations and ensure every team member is aware of their role.

❖ Use Effective Tools - Use online tools that facilitate collaboration and communication. These tools can also aid in sharing ideas and feedback.

Measuring Creative Success

Measuring creative success is essential. Sometimes it is challenging to measure creativity because it causes a ripple effect that is difficult to quantify. Here are some ways to measure creative success:

❖ Use Metrics - Establish metrics such as ROI, customer satisfaction scores, or time/salary saved to track the impact of creative ideas.

❖ Conduct Peer Reviews - Allow others to review the work being done to provide feedback and validate the creativity of the project.

❖ Track Progress - Keep track of the stages of the creative process to monitor progress and evaluate the success of the work.

Conclusion

Creativity is not just a gift that some people are born with. It is a skill that can be developed through experimentation, persistence, and analyzing feedback. The creative process is essential to developing innovative solutions, and it can lead to more significant achievements in any field. By following the guidelines outlined above, anyone can unlock their creative potential and achieve results beyond their wildest imaginations.

CHAPTER 14: STRENGTHENING YOUR FINANCIAL MANAGEMENT SKILLS

As the world becomes increasingly competitive, financial acumen is more critical than ever. Companies that manage their finances well have a greater chance of long-term success. Financial management skills are essential to ensure a business maximizes profits, manages cash flow, and reduces financial risks. This chapter will discuss the basics of financial management, developing a financial plan, managing budgets and cash flow, identifying financial risks, understanding financial statements and ratios, developing cost control strategies, measuring financial performance, and making sound investment decisions.

Understanding the Basics of Financial Management

Financial management is about making informed decisions about financial matters while considering the long-term effects and impact of those decisions. Keeping track of the income and expenses of an individual or business is the first step. Generating financial statements such as balance sheets, cash flow statements, and income statements is the next. These financial statements provide a snapshot of the financial health of a business and act as a foundation for making decisions that impact the organization.

Developing a Financial Plan

Having a well-defined financial plan is key to ensuring the long-term success of a business. Developing a financial plan requires understanding the business's overall goals and strategizing how to achieve those goals financially. A financial plan includes estimating income and expenses, creating a budget, and setting financial objectives. The financial plan serves as a roadmap that outlines the steps necessary to guide the business towards financial success.

Managing Budgets and Cash Flow

Effective budget management is critical for business success. Once a budget has been developed, adhering to it should be a top priority. Budget variance analysis helps businesses determine whether they are staying within budget or deviating from it so they can adjust their spending as needed. Cash flow management is equally important. It ensures that a business has enough cash on hand to pay its expenses and debts, as well as conduct daily operations. Establishing a cash flow forecast can help businesses plan for cash requirements and manage their cash flow.

Identifying Financial Risks

A financial risk is the likelihood of economic loss due to an unexpected event. Companies must identify and manage potential financial risks such as credit risks, market risks, and operational risks. Credit risk refers to the potential for customers to default on their payments. Market risk results from fluctuations in the market. Operational risk results from internal problems such as fraud and errors in financial reporting. Identifying and managing financial risks is imperative for business success.

Understanding Financial Statements and Ratios

Financial statements such as income statements, balance sheets, and cash flow statements provide a snapshot of the financial health of a business. Ratios provide a way to analyze financial statements by comparing two or more aspects of a business's financial performance. These ratios include but are not limited to liquidity ratios, activity ratios, profitability ratios, and solvency ratios. Evaluating financial statements and ratios is critical to understanding the financial health of a business.

Developing Cost Control Strategies

Cost control is an important financial management strategy. Effective cost control strategies enable a business to reduce costs, improve profits, and remain competitive. These strategies can include reviewing procurement and supply chain management to assess whether the business is acquiring goods and services cost-effectively. As well, identifying and addressing areas of waste, reducing supply chain risks, and adjusting prices, if necessary, can assist in mitigating financial risk.

Measuring Financial Performance

One of the best ways to measure financial performance is to carry out a financial analysis. The analysis assesses the business's financial well-being and compares it to industry benchmarks to identify areas of strength and weakness. Regular financial analysis can provide insight into whether the company is generating the intended profits and may identify areas that require further financial attention. Measuring financial performance provides the foundation for making smart financial decisions.

Making Sound Investment Decisions

Making sound investment decisions often involves assessing the potential benefits of an investment with the potential risks. Return on investment (ROI) analysis is a useful tool to help make investment decisions. It is essential to understand the intention of the investment, including whether it is for short-term gains or long-term prosperity. Investment decisions rely heavily on the business's overall financial strategy, including the development of short-term and long-term goals.

Conclusion

In conclusion, this chapter is aimed at developing a strong understanding of financial management, financial planning, managing budgets and cash flow, identifying financial risks, using ratios to assess financial performance, developing cost control strategies, measuring financial performance, and making sound investment decisions. Managing finances is a complex task that can be challenging. Having the essential knowledge, tools, and skills necessary to navigate financial decisions will set you apart in both your personal and business life.

CHAPTER 15: DEVELOPING GLOBAL BUSINESS SKILLS

In today's interconnected world, having an understanding of global business skills is no longer just an added bonus, it's a necessity if you want to succeed. As businesses expand their reach to other nations, there is an increasing need for professionals to have a solid foundation of global business skills. In this chapter, we'll take a closer look at what it means to develop global business skills, why it matters in the current business world, and what steps you can take to strengthen your skillset in this area.

Understanding the Global Business Environment:

Before getting started in building global business skills, it's essential to understand the context in which these skills will be implemented. The global business environment can be unpredictable, complex, and ever-changing. Experts predict that, by 2050, each country will obtain unique comparative advantages, and companies will have to adjust to that reality. In today's era of globalization, businesses often face cross-border collaborations, supply chain challenges, technological advancements, and cultural barriers.

Developing Cross-Cultural Awareness:

One of the most crucial components of global business skills is cross-cultural awareness. It's essential to be open to different cultures and willing to adjust your style to work more effectively with people from diverse backgrounds. To develop cross-cultural awareness, you need to make an effort to learn about other cultures, including their traditions, customs, and beliefs. You can do this through reading, watching documentaries, joining groups that celebrate other cultures, and attending cultural events. By increasing your cultural awareness, you will become more proficient in communicating across various cultures.

Learning to Communicate Across Cultures:

Communication is critical in any business environment, but it becomes an even more significant factor when dealing with different cultures. The ability to communicate effectively across cultures is an essential skill for any professional looking to expand their global business skills. To be successful in this area, it's important to be aware of language barriers and learn how to speak with people who may have limited or no knowledge of your native language. It's also essential to be mindful of different communication styles and learn how to tailor your communication approach to the culture you're dealing with.

Adapting to Different Business Cultures:

In addition to cross-cultural awareness and communication skills, it's also essential to adapt to different business cultures. Each country has unique customs and expectations when it comes to business practices. In some cultures, the pace of business is slow, and decisions are made after a long period of discussion and negotiation. In other cultures, decisions are made quickly, and the pace of business is brisk. Being able to adapt to these cultural differences can be the difference between closing a deal or not. It's crucial to learn how to navigate these cultural differences, and this can be accomplished through research, attending cultural workshops, or speaking with someone who has experience in the local business culture.

Managing Global Teams and Projects:

In today's globalized business world, it's increasingly common to work with teams and projects spread across multiple countries. Managing global teams and projects requires specific skillsets, including excellent communication, effective delegation, and strong teamwork skills. Building trust with your team members, regardless of where they are located, is essential, and can be accomplished through effective communication and team-building exercises. When working with global teams, it's also important to have a clear communication plan and schedule to avoid any miscommunication or delays.

Understanding International Business Law:

When doing business globally, it's crucial to have a solid understanding of international business law. Different countries have different legal frameworks, and it's important to be familiar with the legal requirements of each country you are doing business in. It's essential to consult experts in international law or have an in-house legal professional well-versed in international law. Failing to comply with international laws can lead to legal complications and significant financial losses.

Developing Export and Import Policies:

Exporting and importing goods or services require well-defined processes and protocols. Developing effective policies and procedures for exporting and importing goods or services can help reduce inefficiencies, improve compliance, and avoid legal issues. It's essential to be familiar with international trade agreements, tariffs, export and import regulations, and other requirements. A smooth export or import process can result in increased sales, stronger client relationships, and a competitive edge in the market.

Mitigating Political and Economic Risks:

Doing business in different countries also means that you'll be exposed to a range of political and economic risks. Political instability, natural disasters, and changing regulations can all impact your business. It's important to be aware of the political and economic situation in the countries where you're doing business, and to develop contingency plans to mitigate risks. Researching, networking, and seeking out experts can help you develop strategies to minimize consequences and protect your business.

In conclusion, developing global business skills can give you a competitive edge in today's world of global interconnection. It requires an openness to other cultures, effective communication skills, adherence to international legal frameworks, and an ability to manage teams and projects on a global scale. By honing these skills, you can be better prepared for the challenges and opportunities that come with doing business in an increasingly interconnected world.

CHAPTER 16: LEARNING TO NEGOTIATE EFFECTIVELY

Negotiation is a crucial skill in both personal and professional life. Whether it's a business deal, a salary negotiation, or even a disagreement with a friend or family member, negotiation is a valuable skill that everyone should have. In this chapter, we'll discuss the art of negotiation, what it takes to prepare for a negotiation, and how to close deals successfully.

Understanding the Art of Negotiation

Negotiation is the process of reaching an agreement through discussion and compromise. Negotiation can be challenging, especially when you have to navigate conflicting interests and objectives. Negotiation requires confidence, creativity, and good communication skills.

To negotiate effectively, you need to understand the psychology of negotiation. One of the key behaviors exhibited during a negotiation is the idea of anchoring. Anchoring is when someone sets a starting point or an initial offer. This offer serves as an anchor that shapes the discussions that follow. If you anchor too high, you risk scaring off the other party, and if you anchor too low, you risk leaving money on the table.

Preparing for Negotiation

Effective negotiation requires preparation. You need to research the other party, understand their needs, and know as much as possible about their position. Before going into a negotiation, you should prepare by doing the following:

- ❖ Know your objective: Clearly define what you want to achieve from the negotiation.

- ❖ Know your walk-away point: Identify what you're willing to accept and what you're not willing to concede.

- ❖ Understand the other party's objectives: Try to understand what the other party is trying to achieve and their walk-away point.

- ❖ Plan your opening move: Think of a realistic anchor point that will lead to a successful negotiation.

- ❖ Determine your negotiation style: Choose a style that suits you and the situation, whether it's cooperative, competitive, or a mixture of both.

Developing a Negotiation Strategy

Once you've prepared for a negotiation, it's time to develop a strategy. A negotiation strategy should take into account the information you've gathered and your personal strengths and weaknesses. Your negotiation strategy should consist of these vital elements:

- ❖ Set the tone: Establish a positive tone by acknowledging areas of agreement, sharing common objectives, and creating rapport.

- ❖ Be strategic: Use your research to your advantage, identify the other party's weaknesses, determine your leverage, and identify areas where you can make tradeoffs.

❖ Use persuasive language: Use language that is assertive, but not confrontational. Use "I" statements that communicate your perspective.

❖ Be flexible: Be prepared to make concessions and find a mutually agreeable solution.

❖ Be prepared to walk away: Don't be afraid to walk away if you can't reach a mutually agreeable solution, or if the other party is not working in good faith.

Using Persuasion and Influence

Effective negotiation requires the use of persuasion and influence to sway the other party's perspective. Persuasion and influence can be achieved by doing the following:

❖ Use active listening skills: Listen to the other party's perspective actively and show that you understand their point of view.

❖ Build credibility: Demonstrate your expertise in the topic area and establish your credibility.

❖ Make valid arguments: Use logic and strong arguments that present a persuasive case.

❖ Use social proof: Reference others who have made similar decisions in support of your argument.

❖ Appeal to emotions: Communicate a persuasive story that plays to the other party's emotions.

Overcoming Objections and Resistance

Negotiations often encounter resistance. The key to overcoming resistance is to understand the objections and address them head-on. You can do this by using the following techniques:

- ❖ Ask open-ended questions: Use open-ended questions to uncover the root of the objection.

- ❖ Acknowledge the objection: Validate the other party's concerns and acknowledge their position.

- ❖ Propose solutions: Offer reasonable solutions that address the objections.

- ❖ Use silence: Occasional silence can help you gauge the other party's response and provide time for reflection.

Developing Effective Compromises

Compromising is an essential part of negotiation. To find a solution that works for both parties, you need to be willing to make concessions. Effective compromise requires:

- ❖ Finding common ground: Identify areas of agreement that can be used to find a solution.

- ❖ Tradeoffs: Identify areas where you can make tradeoffs that benefit both parties.

- ❖ Stay focused on the objective: Keep in mind what you're trying to achieve.

Managing Deadlocks and Impasses

Sometimes, a negotiation may reach a dead-end or impasse. If this happens, it's essential to stay calm and use the following techniques:

- ❖ Take a break: Take a short break to allow both parties to reflect.

- ❖ Reframe the discussion: Repeating and attempting to reframe the discussion from a different perspective can help move the negotiation forward.

❖　　Offer alternatives: Propose new options that weren't previously thought about.

❖　　Consider outside help: Outside help, such as a neutral third party, can help to bring fresh viewpoints and possible solutions.

Closing Deals Successfully

The ultimate goal of a negotiation is to close a deal successfully. To do this, you should focus on:

❖　　Confirming the agreement: Make sure both parties understand the terms of the agreement.

❖　Have the agreement in writing: Write down the details of the agreement and have both parties sign it.

❖　　Follow-up: Follow-up after the agreement to ensure that both parties are satisfied with the outcome.

Conclusion

Negotiation is a vital component of both personal and professional life. Effective negotiation requires preparation, strategy, persuasion, and compromise. Knowing how to navigate deadlocks and close deals successfully are the hallmarks of an outstanding negotiator. With these skills, you will be equipped to negotiate successful outcomes in any scenario that comes your way.

CHAPTER 17: NAVIGATING CHANGE MANAGEMENT

Change is a constant in the business world. Whether it's a new product launch, a company restructuring, or a merger or acquisition, organizations must be prepared to navigate change effectively to maintain their competitive edge. Change management is the process of preparing for and implementing changes within an organization while minimizing disruptions to the business. In this chapter, we will explore the process of change management and provide strategies for successfully navigating change in your organization.

Understanding the Process of Change

Before embarking on a change initiative, it's essential to understand the process of change. At its core, change involves moving from one state to another. Typically, change occurs in three stages: the preparation stage, the implementation stage, and the sustainment stage.

The preparation stage involves identifying the need for change and developing a plan for how to make the change effectively. During this stage, it is essential to communicate with stakeholders and garner their support for the change initiative. This stage is critical because it sets the foundation for the success of the change initiative.

The implementation stage involves putting the change plan into action. This stage requires careful planning and execution to minimize disruption to the business. It's also essential to monitor the progress of the change initiative closely and make adjustments as necessary.

The sustainment stage involves ensuring that the changes made are embedded into the organization's culture and processes. This stage requires ongoing monitoring and support to maintain the changes made and prevent the organization from reverting to its old ways.

Developing a Change Management Strategy

To successfully navigate change, it's essential to have a robust change management strategy in place. Developing a change management strategy involves the following steps:

❖ Identify the need for change: The first step is to identify the need for change and why the change is necessary. This will help you to develop a strong case for change and communicate it effectively to stakeholders.

❖ Develop a change management team: The success of a change initiative depends on having a skilled and dedicated change management team in place. The change management team should include stakeholders from all areas of the business and should be responsible for developing and executing the change management plan.

❖ Develop a change management plan: The change management plan should detail the specific steps that will be taken to implement the change, including timelines, milestones, and roles and responsibilities. It's essential to communicate the plan clearly and effectively to all stakeholders to ensure their buy-in and support.

❖ Build support for the change: It's essential to build support for the change initiative across the organization. This can be done by communicating the benefits of the change to stakeholders, addressing their concerns and addressing any resistance to change.

❖ Train employees: Employees must be adequately trained to adapt to the changes and perform their new roles effectively. This may involve providing training on new processes, software, or equipment.

❖ Monitor progress: It's essential to monitor the progress of the change initiative closely and make adjustments as necessary. This will help you to stay on track and mitigate any potential issues.

Communicating Change to Stakeholders

One of the most critical aspects of change management is communication. Effective communication is essential to ensure that all stakeholders are aware of the changes being made and understand their role in the change initiative. Communication should be ongoing and should be tailored to the needs of different stakeholders. It's also essential to address any concerns and resistance to change, and to provide regular updates on the progress of the change initiative.

Building a Change Management Team

As mentioned earlier, the success of a change initiative depends on having a skilled and dedicated change management team in place. The change management team should be responsible for developing and executing the change management plan. The team should include stakeholders from all areas of the business and should have clear roles and responsibilities. The team should be led by a change management expert who has experience in navigating change and can guide the team through the process.

Managing Resistance to Change

Resistance to change is common in any organization. Employees may resist change due to fear of the unknown, a lack of understanding of the change, or a feeling that the change is unnecessary. Managing resistance to change involves the following steps:

❖ Identify the source of resistance: Identify the source of resistance to change and address the employee's concerns or issues.

❖ Communicate the benefits of the change: Communicate the benefits of the change to all stakeholders and how it will impact the organization positively.

❖ Involve employees in the change process: Involve employees in the change process by providing training and support to help them adapt to the changes effectively.

❖ Celebrate successes: Celebrate successes along the way to maintain motivation and support for the change initiative.

Monitoring and Adjusting the Change Process

Monitoring the progress of the change initiative is essential to ensure that it stays on track and meets its goals. It's also essential to make adjustments to the change process as necessary to address any issues or challenges that arise along the way. This may involve revising the change plan, providing additional training, or communicating with employees more effectively. Regular monitoring and adjustment will help to ensure that the change initiative is successful.

Celebrating Successes and Learning from Failures

Finally, it's essential to celebrate successes along the way to maintain motivation and support for the change initiative. Celebrating successes can involve recognizing employees who have contributed to the initiative, providing incentives for progress made, and publicly acknowledging the positive impact of the change. It's also essential to learn from failures and make changes to future change initiatives based on these lessons learned.

Conclusion

Navigating change management can be challenging, but with the right strategy and support in place, it can be a smooth and successful process. Effective communication, building a strong change management team, managing resistance to change, monitoring and adjusting the change process, and celebrating successes, are all essential to ensuring a successful change initiative. As businesses continue to evolve and grow, the ability to navigate change effectively is increasingly indispensable to success.

CHAPTER 18: DEVELOPING ENTREPRENEURIAL SKILLS

Entrepreneurship is a subject gaining immense interest worldwide. As the world becomes more open to new ideas and ventures, being a successful entrepreneur is now among the most prestigious and fulfilling career choices. In this chapter, we will discuss the necessary skills required to establish, operate, and expand your business venture.

Understanding the Entrepreneurial Mindset

Entrepreneurship is a state of mind – an approach to thinking and acting that must be embraced in every aspect of your business. Entrepreneurs are visionary - they do not wait for opportunities to present themselves but rather create opportunities that others may not see. They are risk takers, not afraid to pursue radical changes that can lead to great rewards. Additionally, entrepreneurs are persistent, tenacious, and resilient, recovering quickly from failures while learning valuable lessons to improve their future outcomes.

Identifying Entrepreneurial Opportunities

The first step towards entrepreneurship is to recognize and capitalize on new opportunities. Keep a sharp eye on the world around you for any weakness, flaws, or gaps to be filled. Ask yourself what problems can be solved or what needs your community requires. Identify untapped niches in your field or businesses that have the potential to solve the problems of the status quo. Once you identify an opportunity, analyze how you can leverage it to maximize your chances of success.

Developing a Business Plan

The next crucial step in setting up a business venture is creating a business plan. Your business plan serves as the blueprint for your business, outlining what to expect, how you intend to generate income, and how you will allocate funds to achieve your objectives. A solid business plan should include an executive summary, a description of the products or services you offer, a market analysis, a marketing and sales plan, a breakdown of your operations and management structure, a detailed financial plan and an overview of your legal and regulatory compliance considerations.

Managing Start-up Capital

Before you start a business, you must identify the funds you will require to establish your venture effectively. Depending on the nature of your business, you may require a substantial amount of capital to cover start-up expenses such as rent, equipment, licenses, permits, website development, branding, marketing, and administrative costs. You may also need working capital to sustain your business until you generate adequate revenue to cover your expenses. Once you have determined the capital required, you must seek financing to support your vision, such as loans, crowdfunding or venture capital.

Building an Effective Team

No entrepreneur can build a thriving business alone. As a business owner, building an effective team is crucial to ensure your venture's long-term success. Your team will be your greatest asset in maintaining your business's momentum and growth. To build a strong team, you must first identify the positions necessary to bring your business to life, including the essential skills and qualifications needed for each role. Once you have these in place, you must recruit, train, and motivate your team to maximize their potential and work together towards a common goal.

Developing Sales and Marketing Strategies

Once you have your team, you must create a plan to build a customer base. This plan starts with identifying your target audience and understanding their needs. You must then create a marketing and sales strategy that effectively communicates the value of your products or services. This could include developing a unique branding strategy, establishing social media presence, advertising, cold calling, or even direct mail campaigns.

Measuring Entrepreneurial Success

Entrepreneurial success is measured in various ways. You can track success by monitoring the growth of your business in terms of revenue, profitability, and market share. You can also monitor key metrics such as customer satisfaction, website traffic, leads generated, conversions, and customer lifetime value. Furthermore, you must keep track of your business partners, supporters and community feedback as you scale your business.

Scaling and Growing Your Business

Once your business is up and running, you must look for opportunities to grow and expand. There are various ways to achieve growth, including introducing new products or services, expanding into new geographical regions, adding new sales channels, or extending your brand through franchising. To ensure successful scaling, you must have the necessary capital, infrastructure, and organizational culture to support growth, while keeping the customer experience at the center of your business strategy.

Conclusion

Entrepreneurship is a fulfilling and challenging journey, but the rewards of creating a successful business are immeasurable. This chapter discusses the key factors to consider when starting your own business, from recognizing entrepreneurial opportunities, to building a strong team, to measuring success and driving growth. With these skills, you can navigate the exciting and dynamic world of entrepreneurship and turn your business vision into a reality.

CHAPTER 19: STRIVING FOR WORK-LIFE BALANCE

In today's fast-paced world, it can be easy to get caught up in the hustle and bustle of work, often leading to neglecting other areas of our life. It is crucial to understand the importance of attaining a healthy work-life balance to avoid burnout, stress, and even negative impacts on our physical and mental health. In this chapter, we will explore strategies for achieving the optimal work-life balance.

Understanding the Importance of Work-Life Balance

Work is essential for most individuals to sustain themselves financially, but it should not come at the expense of other areas of their life, such as family, friends, hobbies, and personal growth. Finding the right balance helps to reduce stress, which increases happiness and satisfaction in all areas of our life. It helps individuals to recharge after work, leading to increased productivity and focus when they return to work.

Learning to Manage Stress

Stress is a common problem for many people, and it is essential to learn strategies to manage it effectively. It can lead to a plethora of negative effects on our physical and mental health, including heart disease, high blood pressure, anxiety, and depression. Stress management strategies such as meditation, exercise, and deep breathing can help control stress levels.

Developing Healthy Habits

Developing healthy habits such as eating a balanced diet, drinking enough water, and getting enough sleep are among the most crucial habits to maintain work-life balance. It is critical to prioritize health and wellbeing by incorporating healthy habits into our routine.

Setting Boundaries and Prioritizing Your Time

Setting boundaries and prioritizing tasks can help balance work and personal life. Establishing boundaries means learning to say no when necessary, allocating specific times for activities and keeping personal and work life separate. Prioritizing tasks, focusing on what has to be done instantly and leaving non-urgent assignments for later, will help manage time better.

Learning to Say No

Saying no should not be considered a weak negative response but a healthy way to manage time effectively. It is necessary to understand that overcommitting ourselves to activities ultimately leads to burnout and decreased productivity.

Creating a Support System

Having a supportive family, friends, or colleagues can help balance work and personal life effectively. They can help one another manage time, offer advice on personal and work-related issues, and offer necessary support in difficult situations.

Taking Time Off

Taking some time off work, particularly when there is no urgency, can help reduce stress levels and prevent burnout. Taking a vacation can give employees a chance to rediscover their passions, break from routine, and decompress. Organizations should emphasize the importance of taking time off work as they contribute to overall employee well-being.

Finding Meaningful Pursuits Outside of Work

Engaging in activities and hobbies outside work is essential as it contributes to mental and physical well-being. Pursuing non-work related passions and hobbies can lead to reduces stress levels, increased creativity, improved mental health, and a better outlook on life.

Conclusion

Achieving work-life balance is crucial to overall well-being and happiness. It requires effort, prioritization, and a commitment to manage time effectively. By setting boundaries, prioritizing tasks, saying no when necessary, and creating a support system, employees can achieve work-life balance. It is essential to find healthy ways to manage stress, develop healthy habits, and pursue hobbies and interests outside of work. In conclusion, attaining work-life balance is not an easy task, but with patience and the right strategies in place, it is achievable. Work hard, but don't forget to enjoy the other areas of life.

CHAPTER 20:
CONCLUSION

Congratulations! You have made it to the end of this guide and have hopefully gained some valuable insights and tips for your professional development journey. Let's take a moment to review what you have learned and celebrate your successes.

Throughout this guide, we have explored the various forms of professional development, including assessing your needs, creating a professional development plan, building your professional network, developing leadership, technical and soft skills, mastering project management, improving customer service and satisfaction, learning to innovate, enhancing your presentation skills, cultivating emotional intelligence, strengthening financial management skills, developing global business skills, learning to negotiate effectively, navigating change management, developing entrepreneurial skills, striving for work-life balance, and the importance of continual learning.

You have learned how to identify your strengths and weaknesses, set clear objectives, create a learning schedule, incorporate self-motivation techniques, and time management strategies, and evaluate and adjust your plan accordingly. You have also learned how to build effective relationships and networking, develop emotional intelligence, manage projects, handle customer service, and navigate change successfully.

Remember to celebrate your successes, both big and small. These successes will keep you motivated and on track, ensuring that you continue to grow and develop professionally. It is also essential to identify areas for improvement and to continue striving for excellence. Growth and development are lifelong journeys, and they require a strong commitment to learning and improvement.

Finally, remember to encourage others to develop professionally. Share your knowledge, insights, and experiences with others. As the saying goes, "a rising tide lifts all boats." By encouraging others to develop professionally, you will help to create a community of supportive individuals who are committed to continuous learning and improvement.

Thank you for taking the time to read this guide. I hope that you have found it informative and useful. Remember, your professional development is your responsibility, so continue to invest in yourself and strive for excellence. I wish you all the best on your professional development journey.

ABOUT THE AUTHOR

Ray Goodwin

Ray Goodwin, is the author behind this series of captivating books on Business Development and self improvement, and has left an indelible mark on the field. He was born and raised in the bustling city of London, where he developed a strong work ethic and an insatiable curiosity about the inner workings of successful businesses. Throughout his illustrious career, Ray leveraged his extensive knowledge and experience to help numerous companies flourish and prosper.

His keen insights and innovative strategies has earned him recognition, driving him to share his expertise with others. Ray believes in the power of sharing knowledge to elevate businesses and empower aspiring entrepreneurs.

Ray's dedication to his craft is evident in the numerous books he has authored on business development and self improvement. His writing style seamlessly blends practical advice, thought-provoking concepts, and real-life case studies, making his books invaluable resources for business professionals and novices alike. His ability to distill complex concepts into accessible language has greatly impacted the lives and careers of countless individuals.

Now retired from the corporate world, Ray and his beloved wife have settled in the idyllic English countryside. Surrounded by the beauty of nature, Ray finds inspiration for his writing and indulges in his hobbies.

Ray Goodwin's books continue to serve as enduring guides for those seeking success in the business world. With a wealth of experience and a deep understanding of the inner workings of businesses, Ray's work remains a testament to his passion for sharing knowledge and helping others flourish.

www.ingramcontent.com/pod-product-compliance
Lightning Source LLC
Chambersburg PA
CBHW062354290526
45794CB00005B/2219